DOWNSTREAM

BY

GRACE HAWES

iUniverse, Inc.
New York   Bloomington

Downstream

iUniverse books may be ordered through booksellers or by contacting:

iUniverse
1663 Liberty Drive
Bloomington, IN 47403
www.iuniverse.com
1-800-Authors (1-800-288-4677)

ISBN: 978-1-440-10730-6 (pbk)
ISBN: 978-1-440-10731-3 (ebk)

Library of Congress Control Number: 2008941190

Printed in the United States of America

iUniverse rev. date: 12/31/2008

"By one Chinese view of time, the future is behind you, above you, where you cannot see it. The past is before you, below you, where you can examine it. Man's position in time is that of a person sitting beside a river, facing always downstream as he watches the water flow past...

"In America and other Western countries, the commonest view of abstract time seems to be the opposite of the old Chinese one. In this, man faces in the other direction, with his back to the past, which is sinking away behind him and his face [is] turned upward to the future, which is floating down upon him... He is more like a man in a plane than a sitter by a river."

<u>Two Kinds of Time</u> by Graham Peck

This is dedicated

To my

Darling

Grandchildren

Whose eyes are

Focused

Upstream

The following list of previously published poems was inadvertently left out of <u>The Turtle Tattoo</u>, a book of my poetry published in 2006.

"Visitation", <u>Fire</u> 19, January 2003

"Mantra", "Summer of '42", "Perspective", "California Dreamin'", "Love Song", <u>Fire</u> 25, March 2005

"Windfall", <u>Fire</u> 26, September 2005
plus, in this collection
"The Haesemeyers", <u>Reflections,</u> 2008
<u>Fire</u> is a British poetry magazine and <u>Reflections</u> is published in Oregon

TABLE OF CONTENTS - DOWN-STREAM

PALS

My grandfather

drives the team

of slow horses pulling the

farm wagon

when we

ride into town

for supplies

and ice cream cones

WISCONSIN SPRING

In the north woods this year

    white trillium blossoms

    cover the ground

Not quite as many

    as the wild flowers

    John Muir crushed

    with every step

    in a California valley

But close

MESSAGE

My mother's hands were strong

    farm girl hands

    impervious

    in every season

    except winter

    when tiny cracks

    appeared in her

    chapped fingertips

Even then

        her hands looked strong

            the way we always

            expected her to be

        Only later did we realize

        the vulnerable fingertips

        were closest to her truth

ASSIMILATION

Slim Jim and the Vagabond Kid

        were on the radio in the '30's

        singing cowboy songs in their

        thick

        just-off-the-boat

        Norwegian accents

For their adoring audiences in

        Minnesota and Wisconsin

        they were as authentic as if they'd been

      REAL cowboys of the old American West

Riding horses
      in a Texas round-up
Herding cattle
      across the open prairie
Hanging around
      the old corral

Ya Ya
      you betcha by golly

ON BEING EIGHT YEARS OLD

Not a sound

Not a wisp of air

I lie on the grass

transcendent

in the August heat

A cloud floats slowly overhead

and one tiny drop of rain

falls on my cheek

Summer is mine

GRADE SCHOOL

We climbed the zigzagging
     fire escape all the
     way to the top
        where the railing was missing
and we had to stay close to
the brick wall to feel safe

We went up the wide oak staircase
        to the fourth floor that was
        empty and no longer used

Higher still, we climbed all the way to the
        cupola that held the school bell
where we could look down on the
treetops and the houses
        all the way to the lake

When the venerable Victorian
            built to last forever
     came down
     to make way
     for an efficient
     nondescript one-story structure

     we mourned

We knew
     a school building that
     inspired both curiosity
     and exploration
        could never be replaced

BLIND-SIDED

One time as a kid

    I ate so many apples

    I got hives

Overindulging

    even in a good thing

    can backfire

COME INTO MY PARLOR

At dusk

water lilies

look like a patterned carpet

inviting you to take the first step

DOUBLE DARE YOU

The game was called "Jumping Off the Garage Roof"

    I tried it once

When I hit the ground

    the impact rattled up my spindly legs

    all the way to my shoulders

    and into my head

where I was sure it had

    jerked my brain loose

The other kids did it over and over

    egging me on

    calling me names when I refused

They jumped and jumped until our neighbor looked out the window

    and yelled STOP

I was grateful

    Paper dolls were more my forte

AMENITIES

Our sheets smelled of fresh air

even in winter

when they froze on the line

and hung like stiff white boards

'til dry

Always

they brought us the

out-of-doors

the wind and sun of Northern woodlands

unforgettable
delicious

Now

fresh air and sunshine

aren't involved

Modern conveniences
sad to say

don't play to the senses

HOME REMEDY

A child's bare foot slips

        into a lakeside

        clay bed

        and provides an

        unexpected snack

        for a nest of baby leeches

A hundred years earlier

        the mother might

        have considered

        leeches beneficial

Not today

She dispels the unwanted and

        soothes the injured

        with one swift and simple treatment

A generous sprinkling of salt

IT'S TIME

Bears tread slowly over

patches of lingering snow

not yet fully awake

except for a raging appetite

that tells them it's spring

CINEREOUS

All the photos

    my dad took

    with his old camera

      black and white

    were actually shades of gray and white

A subtler world than the one we knew

POWER DRINK

Our lake is five miles long

and on a winter day

we skate on its bumpy surface

to a cabin

where last summer's

apple juice

frozen to slush

tastes like ambrosia

and fortifies us for the

five miles back

NON COMPOS MENTIS

Sleeping on your

    mother's shoulder

    as she rocks you

    back and forth

is as secure as you'll ever get

How could we know

HEAL THYSELF

Our grandmother had
  illnesses we'd never
  heard of

  quincy
  catarrh
  lumbago
  the grippe

Illnesses she diagnosed and treated
  and from which
    for almost ninety years
  she unfailingly recovered

To her
  doctors were for the end
  not the journey

LESSON

It's unlikely that the
    piece I'd practiced
    all week was Ingolf Dahl's "Reflection"
    but it should have been
As I waited my turn
    in Mrs. Lange's living room
        for my piano lesson to begin
I amused myself
    by making faces
    at the lady
    reflected in the hallway mirror
        eyes crossed
        tongue stuck out
        ears flapped
        nostrils flared
    every insulting facial distortion
    my ten-year-old brain could conjure
until
the lady herself appeared in the doorway
    came toward me with a stern look
        and said

"Don't you know that when you see
    someone in a mirror, they can see you, too?"

"Oh," I said in a tiny embarrassed voice

But even before the humiliation vanished
    I was relishing
    this amazing bit of information

"Reflection" may not have been
    my piano solo that week
    but it was enduringly
my lesson

17

SOIL AERATION

Almost seventy years later

       we remember
          the mantra of our
              high school biology teacher

"Earthworms," he told us
     over and over
"are man's best friend."

Repetition
     sometimes
     aerates the mind

A PET TO HUG

I begged for a dog

We got a canary

Parents
      at times
            just don't *get* it

DRAWBRIDGE

We grew up on an island

    surrounded by a glacier-excavated moat

    that kept us

    barricaded and safe

until the War

    when even on our remote island

    the world found us

CAN WINTER BE FAR BEHIND

Every autumn

    fallen leaves were

    raked and burned in bonfires

    all up and down our street

A rite of the season

    banished now

    by the ozone layer

Yet the smell of

    burning leaves

    imprinted in

        memory's ashes

    lingers in the

        air of September

SHE WAS OUR HOME

Ladies Aid met at the
    church once a month

Mother always attended

I don't know what they "aided"
    but it wasn't my sister or me

What a letdown to burst in the door
    from school
        with tales of the day's great
        adventures and

alas

Just an empty house and a
    lost forlorn feeling

Once a month only
    and we could barely
    do without her

POLITICS

Every Friday

    in fourth grade

    two boys

    sang

      "Home on the Range"

Every single Friday

    the same song

My friend Lois and I knew

    the latest hits

      from the radio

      and the movies

Every week a different song

Nascent sides of the political spectrum

    Our duets foretold

    Our future

IMPROV

"Cinderella's Married Life" was

a play we made up and performed

on a neighbor's back porch

Poor Cinderella

We did not present

her life as

happily ever after

The Prince yelled and stomped

an impromptu performance

that brought Cinderella to tears

"I'm going home," she sobbed

"Go," said the Prince, imperiously, and

pushed her off the porch

where she

scraped her knees and ran home crying

The audience applauded

SUMMER VACATION

It's good to know what it feels like

> to run downhill as
> hard and fast as you can

to skinny-dip at night .
> in the silken water of
> a sun-warmed lake

to tip over a friend's canoe
> in the pouring rain
> and laugh hysterically
> until you right it
> and crawl back in

to talk for hours with friends
> and never ever
> run out of things to say

to wake up for school
> and remember

it's July

CATALYST

Diane believes

     that everyone she knows
     should be friends
     with everyone else
she knows

No matter that we have
     absolutely

     nothing

     in common

In Diane's mind

     we do

And before long
     it happens
     quite unintentionally

We become friends
     and stay friends

Because
     to disappoint to disavow Diane

     would be

     unthinkable

SELF-RIGHTEOUS SYNTAX

Annoyed, I say to
    my obstreperous three-year-old

"I DO wish you'd behave."

Looking up at me defiantly
    with justice clearly on his side

he retorts,

"I AM being have."

HOME SWEET HOME

A lichen and moss-covered

rock

provides

a rich landscape

for a multitude

of tiny scuttering

residents

FOODIE

World travel is wonderful
known to educate
forgotten soon are jet lag
and planes that leave too late

Monuments so ancient
castles on the hills
museums without number
scenes that give you chills

And there is something else
that lingers
in my mind
as years go by
the new cuisine in every country
exotic food I get to try

If an army travels on its stomach
as Napoleon did state
I too remember always
whatever's on my plate

MATERIALISM

Enough never is

SIDE BY SIDE

On a soft summer evening
      in the English countryside

American tourists step off a bus
      and follow their guide
      across a wide meadow of
      tall dew-covered grass

      soon aware that their
      unmarked footpath is
      land-mined
      with copious evidence
      of a cowherd that has
      only recently
      moved on

Uttering only an occasional
      barely heard expletive
      the visitors zigzag toward
      a line of folding chairs

Once there
      they sit quietly
      awed by the serene twilight beauty and
      admiring
            across the vast expanse
            of precisely mown lawn

      an ancient castle
Few of the visitors had heard of the ceremony they'd
come to see

Beating Retreat (the guidebook said)
the signal at sunset for soldiers to stop
fighting
the oldest battle tradition of the British
Army

Exactly on time
    from the far side of the castle
    drums sounded
    and young men
            splendid in brilliant red uniforms
            perfectly matched like toy soldiers
            march to a slow rolling beat

    Drums, fifes, 'pipes
            bringing to life
            past empire and glory

The visitors watch
    spellbound

            only now and then aware
            of the scent of cow dung
            wafting up
            from their shoes

Unmindful that

    as so often happens in life

the glorious and the mundane

are capriciously

juxtaposed

PAVE PARADISE

The orchard

across the street

owned by the same family for

almost a hundred years

was bulldozed and gone in a day

Acres of trees soon

replaced by acres of houses

"It's progress," they said

We missed the trees

BORN AGAIN

I open my eyes
    and for
        one tiny moment
before I'm fully awake

everything from yesterday
    and all the yesterdays
    has vanished

OUT OF THE MOUTHS OF BABES

She was six

    going out the door

    to school

"It's cold," I say

    "Here's your sweater."

"I'm not wearing it."

"Put it on."

"No."

"You might as well give up.
    You know I'll win the battle."

She grabs the sweater

Then over her shoulder
    as she goes down the walk
she calls back to me

"You might win the battle, but
    I'll win the war."

I stand and stare

Little does she know how profoundly
    right she is

BY WAY OF EXPLANATION TO
MY SON JOHN WHO
WHEN HE HAD NOTHING TO DO WAS ADMONISHED
TO "GO COLOR"

After Dick Quinn splashed
    lemonade on the
    dining room wallpaper
    at my 8th birthday party
boys were banned from
    our house

Friends at school

    but not at home

So I never really
    learned that
    boys don't want
    to sit quietly
    and stay in the lines

I was sure you'd *like* to color
    once you got the hang of it

I'm so sorry

    but you see

it was all Dick Quinn's fault

BOOKS (FOR MARIAM WHO ONCE TOLD ME SHE HATED TO READ*)

Books are better than
Booze
Shoes
New age blues

Larks
Parks
Just found quarks

Bikes
Hikes
Sautéed pikes

Apes
Grapes
Cashmere capes

Ale
Kale
First-class mail

Sex
Pecs
Hot TexMex

Books rock

*She likes to read now. Probably because of this poem.

CONDOS

We hear them

   living their lives

       footsteps
       music
       quarrels
       laughter
       greetings
       farewells

Communal living it's called

   but only the sounds

  of our neighbors are familiar

     The emanations of strangers

ESPLANADE

Benches made of redwood

    hard

    enduring

designed for some

    ideal human form

Inhospitable seating

    for the daily inhabitants

        none of them ideal

All of them

    willing to pay the

    price of discomfort

    to sit for hours

        watching the sea perform

DARJEELING

All the characters in the book I've just put down

    every one

is struggling

against 21st century odds

and although

    half a world away

    we've reaped most of the benefits

we too suffer the ravages

TURNING POINT

In one of the first busloads
        of tourists
        allowed into China
        after thirty years of
        Mao-imposed isolation

we were thrilled at last to see the
        country we had studied for so long

Our young guide
        who told us he'd
        been a Red Guard
        a few years earlier

was just as thrilled to meet us
        these strange-looking foreigners
and to practice his textbook English

Especially
        he said
he wanted to learn
        American songs

To our surprise
        the first song we taught him
        seems to have swept the country

                The Chinese have been living it ever
                since

And what was that history-changing song?

        We taught him "We Shall Overcome"

THE END

Love is lost

    when the need to be separate

        subsumed
        in order
        to please
        to conquer

    reappears and overwhelms

CHANGE OF LIFE

Involutionary melancholia
they called it
and they took you away

After the shock treatments
they brought part of you back

The other part never returned

REST STOP

We drift off to sleep

listening to the

music of a

fast-flowing stream

after a five-hundred-mile day

in a station wagon

loaded with luggage

toys and kids

ELLY AND I

We could have gone to Hollywood
    and become actresses

We could have
    joined the Army
    and served our country in the War

We could have learned Russian
    and become spies

We could have studied epidemiology
    and fought world pandemics

We could have become paleontologists
    and discovered the first humans
    in Africa

The possibilities were endless when we were twenty

As it turned out
    we did none of the above

But if you think all the possibilities are gone
    think again

Our grandchildren might do any or all of the above

    And that counts too

KEGGER

Every year when the

    pyracantha berries

    are aged and fermented

the robins indulge

    until the backyard

    is full of birds drunkenly

    staggering in flight

The next day

    both birds and berries are gone

    until a year from now

    when they get together again

WHERE'S DALE CARNEGIE
WHEN I NEED HIM

The audience is waiting

I step forward

and

in a voice I've never heard before

begin to turn

these innocent people

into victims

of my fright

LITERATURE

We'd like life

to be

a long exciting

novel

Or a lyric poem

with joyous love

and

no sadness

Or a play in three long acts

with a happy ending

But mostly it's

a short story

developed quickly

only momentarily

savored and

over too soon

FAN

Whether I'm spending the

        dime it cost when I was a kid

Or the ten dollars today

        as long as I can totter
        to my seat with a
        bag of popcorn

I'll go to the movies

Netflix and Turner Classics
        are fine

But nothing compares
        with the flutter
        of excitement

when the lights go down

and I am submerged in shadows
        and imagination

SORROW

The words I

wrote in tears

years ago

cannot be read again

 without reviving the indelible sadness

 and more bitter tears

IN THE GOBI DESERT

There were five of us
    that morning

stepping onto the beat-up van
    glancing at the spare parts under the seats
    and the extra can of gasoline

We smile hesitantly at the driver
    who speaks Chinese and a Uighur
    dialect
    and find a place to sit on the tattered seats

With reassuring gestures in our direction
    he starts the van and
    heads straight into a landscape of
    bleak gray rocks and sand

    as far as the eye can see

There is no road
    no path
    no trail

He must know where he's going
    we assure one another

Hours go by

We bump along forlorn terrain
    the only sign of life

    a few camel tracks in the sand
    and one small lizard

at last

    when we're certain

    we'll be robbed and abandoned

the driver points far into the distance

and on the horizon
    we see what remains
    of a great empire's westernmost
    outpost

the ancient gate where

    over a thousand years ago

    legendary caravans passed on their way to
      Bukhara
      Samarkand
      Antioch

    carrying silk for the Middle East

    bringing back horses for Chinese warriors
      perfume for their ladies

Crumbled ruins

Yet in the desolate beauty

    of the ancient passageway

    the romantic mystique of the

    Silk Road remains

IN THE GOBI DESERT II

Before we get in the van to return

    the driver motions for us to follow him

We step inside a small

    unmarked building and cannot believe our eyes

In this place
    as remote and uninhabited
    as the other side of the moon

there is that ubiquitous fixture

    of tourist attractions

    around the world —

    there is a *Gift Shop*

Today we will

    take with us a once-in-a-lifetime

    Silk Road memory

    and each of us
        will also
        get back on the bus
        with a sackful of
        souvenirs

BRIEF ENCOUNTER

Last night I dreamed about

    an old boyfriend

We were at a party

I recognized him

    even though the

    curly blonde hair he hated anyone to touch

    is gone

We hugged
    remembering

Yet when I asked about

    his five brothers

    he looked pained

CONDOLENCE

Words of comfort

diminish

in direct proportion

to the depth

of the tragedy

CAN'T PUT IT DOWN

Sometimes when I'm reading

I can almost hear my mother
calling to me,

"Go to bed, Grace.
It's late."

"OK, mother, just one more chapter."

Just
one
more
chapter

Four words
to
live by

EVERYONE SAYS THEY HAVE A SMART DOG BUT WE REALLY DO

You know I don't want you to do that

    I say to the dog

    when he walks on my

    newly scrubbed floor

With a look

    he turns on his heel and leaves the room

I never have to tell him twice

    Now that's smart

OH HAPPY DAY

On a cloudless

California Sunday

    with the sound of a rainbird

    chuffing in the background

the kind man's voice on the phone

says he wishes

    to publish

    my manuscript

MAGNANIMITY

My sister and cousin
    not long ago
    mentioned that I was
    very bossy
    when we were kids

Obviously
    they didn't appreciate
    my responsibility
    as the eldest

        to guide
        to teach and
        to discipline from time to time
            with a shove or a pinch

It was after all *always*
    for their own good

SERENDIPITY

I was mad at
    all of them

    husband
    children
dog

Can't remember why
    but furious enough to
    slam the door
    get in the car
    and take off

But what to do
    where to go

One or another of them were
    always with me

A movie?
    Of course
        No idea what's playing
        Don't care

But it turned out I had a perfect choice

The movie I saw that afternoon
    just happened to be

    "Diary of a Mad Housewife"

LOVE

Compassion stirs
my heart
begetting love

WHAT'S WRONG WITH THIS PICTURE

Life is mined

    with chaos

    disorder

    and indigestion

when what we long for and often expect

    are harmonious reason

    calm control

    and body peace
        (even if we've just eaten
        raw garlic and jalapeños)

MT. HOOD

Clouds like a
      dancer's shimmering
      veils

drift past

revealing
      only enough
      to tantalize

THE HAESEMEYERS

There were five

    of them

        standing in the bitter Wisconsin cold

        singing carols

and in a basket

          for us

the welcome gift of

            warm homemade food

The year my mother died

    they were our only Christmas

YOUTH

It's departure revises

OLD AGE

It's arrival surprises

WISHFUL THINKING

I always wanted

Our country

To be the Mother Teresa

Of nations

FAREWELL

Walking across the

marble floor

through the huge oak doors

    I'd entered

        years earlier

I know

    nothing

    will ever be

    the same

POETRY REDUCTION

From three pages

sometimes five

to a paragraph

Reduced like a

wine sauce for lamb

Hoping to be as tasty

PETER PAN

In second grade
        one of my classmates
                brought a book to school to share

The book was filled with
        beautiful illustrations in
        shades of palest
        green that
        floated off the pages
        into my imagination

Avarice stirred my little heart

        I *wanted* that book

But when my classmate
        took it home
        I never saw it again

Years later

        I told my daughter about

        those unforgettable illustrations

        and how I'd coveted that long-remembered book

Before the week was out

        she showed up on my doorstep and handed it to
        me

Amazon dot com makes dreams come true

REQUIEM

A folded flag is placed in my arms

on a March day

as my children and I

stand together

alone

HAIKU

Chiaroscuro autumn

Alone and lonely

Chocolate to the rescue

SOMNOLENCE

We drift in the boat as the

sun goes down

and from

across the lake

    a loon calls

YOU GOTTA LOVE 'EM

Even though

    AARP recruits them

    and their hair is gray

the California boomers

    still think

    death is optional

REMEMBRANCE

They were in love

   when they read

      "For a long time, I used to...."

Three volumes later

   they parted

knowing they'd had the

   best

      of both

literature and love

ANATOMY

High arches

make

beautiful footprints

THE KINDNESS OF
STRANGERS

This morning I was
    driving very slowly
    searching for a parking
    space on Capitola's esplanade

The impatient pick-up driver
    behind me
    gave a prolonged angry blast
    on his horn

From the sidewalk
    across the way
    a female voice
    called out to him

"Relaaaaax, asshole!!"

***

How endearing to
    have a stranger
    come to my defense
    with an oxymoron of
    unimaginable perfection

And
    the best laugh I've had in ages

JOB SECURITY

Each and every one of us
      has two dates
            on the calendar

            one to begin
            one to end
In between
      a minor punctuation mark
      represents our lifetime

It is the most important
      work that the
      nearly invisible *dash*
      is ever asked to do

HIGH SCHOOL REUNION

All the years

in between

altered

the shells

but not the

pearls

AVERAGE

We slide along

    the edges of life

        conforming

        not making waves

        or headlines

Content to hide in

    Warren Harding's "normalcy"

the sturdy foundation

on which others

build empires

RECONCILABLE DIFFERENCES?

Once

    I loved feeling

        safely enveloped in pea soup fog

    I loved giant snowflakes

        on my tongue

    I loved being soaked to the skin

        in summer rain

The weather and I were friends

But somewhere along the way

    we separated and began to avoid

    one another's company

Why did we drift apart? Were we incompatible?

    I'm not sure

Next time I have a chance

I'm going to try a snowflake or two

and see if we can't get back together

OOPS

When a friend

    recalling

    the death of Czech leader

    Jan Masaryk

said, "He died of defenestration."

I replied, "Wait a minute. Are you sure?

    I thought he fell out a window."

LAST CHAPTER

Our tales

are of the past

all the good sad humorous

details of life already lived

retrieved in the telling

LONGING

Every September

    as they arrive on campus

I long

    for a moment

    to join them

To be a freshman again

    arriving in Madison on the train

        from way up North

    coming from a high school with two hundred students

        to a university with twelve thousand

    the first in my family to go to college

    a country bumpkin like Jude

    hopes high

    dreams unlimited

Rarely

    do I wish to relive

    part of my past

But for a moment

    every September...

CHIAROSCURO

Every human heart

has a dialectic archive of

sorrow and joy

what was and what might have been

ROMANCE IN THE TIME OF ELDERNESS

They'd known each other
      for years

and at one point
      toyed with the idea
      of having a love affair

but by then
      naps interfered with
      afternoon trysts

and since neither of them could drive now
      clandestine rendezvous
      in discreet motels
      were out

So with the ease of accumulated years
      they remained
      quite happily
      just good friends

AFTERTHOUGHT

"Better to burn out

       than rust out"

I used to say

but lately

after accumulating a

good deal of rust

I've altered my priorities

HOW KIND IT IS

Memory

    filters

    revises

    enhances

and

    while acknowledging moments of deepest sorrow

still manages to

convince us

we've lived a charmed life

Photo credit: Diane Ericksen 2007